I T MAY NOT B[...] time to chara[...] of philanthropy [...], overall U.S. charitable giving, at nearly $300 billion, is close to a record level – and the percentage of the nation's economy devoted to it is (at 2.2 percent) twice that of the next closest nation (the United Kingdom, at 1.1 percent). What's more, philanthropy has been enthusiastically embraced by a new generation of the very wealthy. Led by Bill Gates and Warren Buffett, some 92 billionaires have signed on to the Giving Pledge – to donate more than half their fortunes to good causes over the course of their lifetime.

Yet below the surface, the traditions of philanthropy, individual charity, and the organizations they support are facing both sustained intellectual criticism and policy proposals that could significantly limit them. Note the use of the term *independent philanthropy* – by which I mean charitable giving directed, perhaps even conceived, by its donor. It is this independence that is under fire. Serious critics assert that unless charity is directly "redistributionist" – meaning that the wealthy transfer asserts to organizations that directly assist the poor – it's not really charitable at all. In addition, there are public policy proposals, including one from the Obama White House – that would erode the value of the long-standing tax incentive for charitable giving or limit it to select purposes. Finally, there has even emerged what can be termed government-led philanthropy – in which Washington chooses both goals and organizations and actively calls for private donors to direct their funds toward matching those same priorities. This follows decades, beginning in the 1960s, when nonprofit charitable organizations that were founded to serve those in need came increasingly to work under contract to the government, rather than relying on private donations.

In short, there is decreasing contemporary support for, and a diminishing awareness of, the tradition of what can be called independent philanthropy – charitable giving directed by donors themselves (or their agents) not in partnership with or at the direction of government but rather at their own discretion. It's the sort of giving that one of the first important American philanthropists, Andrew Carnegie, had in mind when he wrote of the

---

Philanthropy and even the smallest gifts of individual charity have a deep relationship with and a promotion of democratic values.

---

benefits that accrue when "the surplus wealth of the few will become, in the best sense, the property of the many, because administered for the common good, and this wealth, *passing through the hands of the few,* can be made a much more potent force for the elevation of our race than if it had been distributed in small sums to the people themselves" *(emphasis added)*. The goal, wrote Carnegie, is for philanthropy to succeed in the "difficult and serious task" of "wise distribution."

I want to make a case for this sort of independent philanthropy and will focus on three key attributes of such giving and what it enables. First – notwithstanding charges of elitism – philanthropy and even the smallest gifts of individual charity have a deep relationship with and a promotion of democratic values. They are not only in keeping with democracy, but they also help strengthen it. Second, their importance is, what's more, practical as well as theoretical. Independent philanthropy can embody imagination and creativity; it can have the courage to disdain conventional wisdom and recognize and address social needs. Third, even when it eschews partnership with government, it has, nonetheless, the ability to reach broadly and effectively by influencing the norms of values and behavior.

In short, to the extent that America continues to rein in the independence of philanthropy, we do so at our own risk.

The traditions of philanthropy and individual charity and the organizations that they support are deeply established in the culture of the United States. Famously, Alexis de Tocqueville, writing in 1840, could observe, "Americans of all ages, all conditions, and all dispositions, constantly form associations ... of a thousand other kinds – religious, moral, serious, futile, excessive or restrictive, enormous, or diminutive.... In this manner they found hospitals, prisons, and schools."

Indeed, so well established was this tradition that virtually from the time the federal income tax was established, in 1913, provision was made (in 1917) for the tax deductibility (and thus a decrease in tax liability) of contributions to nonprofit charitable organizations. Members of Congress were concerned that prominent organizations such as the American Red Cross would face reductions in support, demonstrating that major nationally known nonprofits were already a feature of American life and that their support was broad-based. As a report of the Joint Committee on Taxation has put it, the deduction "was viewed as an effective way to distribute public money to charities, as it cut out the government middlemen. Many believed charities could deliver social services better than the government and that it was appropriate for individuals rather than the government to decide which charities to support."

The accomplishments of American philanthropy are too extensive to list. They include the libraries of Andrew Carnegie, the universities founded by John D. Rockefeller and Leland Stanford, the "green revolution" agricultural breakthroughs supported by the Ford Foundation, and, more recently, the breakthroughs in medical and genetic research enabled by the Broad Foundation and others. Nonetheless, in the present era of dramatically greater government spending on social services than was the case in 1917, as well as persistent federal deficits and growing public debt – to which the tax deduction for charitable giving makes a modest contribution – the American philanthropic tradition has come under fire.

The criticisms are multiple. It's said that philanthropy is undemocratic precisely because, as the Joint Committee stated, it reduces donors' tax liability (and thus federal revenues) while permitting them to decide, on their own and with little oversight, where their funds should be directed. A related criticism asserts that many organizations receiving philanthropic support do not serve those demonstrating the greatest economic need – owing, as one critic has said, to a "pattern of giving that appears hard to reconcile with redistributive outcomes." In other words, philanthropy's favorable tax treatment reduces tax revenue that would otherwise be put to purposes more beneficial to the public. Even scholars who are sympathetic to the mission of the nonprofit institutions for which charitable donations are the lifeblood view such giving as most defensible when it supports organizations that are also the beneficiaries of government grants and contracts. According to this view, the reach of charitable nonprofits is best extended by the use of public funds to supplement private, charitable resources and thereby extend their reach through a partnership with the government.

How did the U.S. reach the present point in the discussion about the role and legitimacy of philanthropy? To appreciate the current debate, one must look at the extent of current charitable giving and its uses. But one must also look back at the gradual narrowing of the independent role of philanthropy and the substitution and supplementation of its role with government appropriations – as well as at a series of influential arguments as to why this should be so. Historical momentum, it might be said, has moved inexorably toward questioning the value and legitimacy of independent philanthropy – even to the point, today, of calls for only certain types of charitable gifts to qualify for favorable tax treatment.

The role of charitable donations – what they fund and the public policies affecting them –

is not a small matter in the United States. Americans donate nearly $300 billion (in 2011, it was $298 billion) annually to organizations qualifying for the charitable tax deduction (nonprofits) – a sum exceeding that of any other country in absolute terms and as a share of GDP. In 2005, for instance, Americans donated more than twice the amount, as a percentage of GDP (2.2 percent), than did the next closest Organisation for Economic Co-operation and Development country (the United Kingdom, at 1.1 percent). The donations support a range of purposes so broad that the Giving USA Foundation, the definitive source for such data – and itself a nonprofit – groups them into no fewer than eight major types, some of which are themselves composites: religion; education; human services; health; public-society benefit; arts, culture, and humanities; international affairs; environment; and animals.

Moreover, philanthropy continues to be seen by the wealthiest individual Americans as a responsibility and even an obligation.

Philanthropy continues to be seen by the wealthiest individual Americans as a responsibility and even an obligation.

Consider the language of the Giving Pledge, through which those 92 American billionaires said that they would "commit to giving the majority of their wealth to the philanthropic causes and charitable organizations of their choice either during their lifetime or after their death." (The pledge was first announced in 2010 by Bill Gates and Warren Buffett.) But charitable giving in the United States today is hardly limited to the superrich. Giving by that group, extensive as it is, still pales next to what the historian Olivier Zunz has called "mass philanthropy," as detailed by Giving USA, which reports that some "117 million households across America ... 12.4 million corporations that claim charitable deductions, an estimated 99,000 estates, and about 76,000 foundations" make donations totaling nearly $300 billion to about "1.1 million IRS-registered charities, plus a conservative estimate of 222,000 American religious organizations."

The existence of a tradition so broadly based and deeply established, as well as ongoing blue-chip endorsements of it, seems to indicate little need to promote or defend independent American philanthropy. Actual giving, moreover, after dipping during the 2007–08 financial crisis, has begun to recover. None of this should be taken as a sign that public policy as it relates to philanthropy is a settled matter. Whether some philanthropic purposes are more desirable than others, whether philanthropy is an appropriate or adequate response to important social problems, and whether and how government should use the tax code to encourage general philanthropy, or only certain types of philanthropy, are controversial matters today in the United States.

It is a controversy with roots that go back at

least a century. During that time, the nation has changed from one in which charitable organizations were the dominant means of addressing social ills to one in which government – and organizations funded by it – has taken the lead. It is no exaggeration to say that independent philanthropy has been steadily under fire and that the most influential policy arguments have been those mounted against it, rather than in its defense.

Indeed, the question of the value of charitable giving – and the related question of what sorts of aid to the poor and distressed should be funded or directly provided by the government – is not a new one. It is central to Amos Griswold Warner's classic 1894 book, *American Charities: A Study in Philanthropy and Economics.* Warner described what was then a vast network of private charities – religious, secular, ethnic – that cared for widows and orphans, arranged for foster care ("placing out"), operated "industrial" schools to train the poor, offered instruction in English for immigrants, and, in times of distress, provided a "dole" for the poor (but not, it was hoped, for "paupers" – those considered at risk of becoming dependent on charity). Focusing on his home city of Baltimore as a case in point, Warner found there were some "120 private charitable institutions or societies" including many "of wide influence" – linked by a central coordinating system common in major cities of the era, the Charity Organization society.

It was Warner's working assumption in the late 19th century that private, philanthropically supported organizations were the default means of providing most social services, except under limited and specific circumstances and involving routinized care. He specifically noted care for the insane, the deaf, dumb, blind, and the epileptic.

For Warner, this was a fact of life – something to be understood and not particularly criticized. By the early 20th century, however, charitable giving by the extremely wealthy had begun to become controversial.

Carnegie and Rockefeller faced the challenge of convincing a skeptical public that their good works on a grand scale (hundreds of public libraries, the establishment of the University of Chicago) amounted to more than image polishing on the part of men whose business practices were not universally admired. The foundations they founded would, in time, win admiration. But other early 20th century criticisms of charity and philanthropy would prove potent. It was then that new voices emerged that called, for the first time, for government to be the default provider of support for those in need who are affected by such conditions as unemployment and old-age poverty. I. M. Rubinow, a physician who decided that he could do more for the poor by advocating for government-provided health insurance, old-age pensions, and unemployment compensation and other "social insurance" (the title of his 1913 book), was specifically disdainful of philanthropy. He dismissed charity as an objectionable expedient, with "its insufficiency," "degrading character," and "social injustice." Wrote Rubinow: "A sickness insurance law even in one state can do more to eradicate poverty and is, therefore, a greater social gain, than a dozen organizations for scientific philanthropy, with their investigations, their sermons on thrift, and their constant feverish hunt for liberal contributions."

Rubinow's triumph would come in the 1930s, when charity as the first line of support for those in economic distress was, as a practical matter, discredited. Herbert Hoover has been judged harshly by history for insisting, even in the depths of the Depression, that the government refrain from providing direct financial relief to those in need, and even for resisting the idea that government funds might be distributed by private charitable groups, such as the Red Cross, which made it known that it would not accept government funding "on principle." Hoover, writes historian Olivier Zunz, was anxious "to avoid direct government support of relief. He feared it would dry up private charity." The subsequent passage of the Social Security Act, signature legislation of the Roosevelt administration, brought Rubinow's vision of government-led social insurance for the most common exigencies – such as unemployment and poverty among the elderly – to fruition.

Indeed, in the years since, Americans have come to the political consensus that income support for the unemployed and the elderly, as well as the working poor, is very much the province of government. The Depression cemented the idea that philanthropy and charitable organizations were fundamentally inadequate to deal with the most dire economic crises faced by typical Americans. Automatic government-provided, so-called countercyclical safety-net programs of income support not only protect those in need but are believed to soften economic downturns. These programs include unemployment compensation, food stamps, and the Earned Income Tax Credit (an income supplement for the working poor). Arguably, government is the most efficient administrator of such programs (although they are not without fraud and abuse) that are very large and that enjoy wide support. Warner might well consider such income-support programs as so well suited to standardization and not demanding high levels of personal attention, so as to be appropriately provided by the government. Put another way, *if* Americans choose to use the tax system to redistribute income, having the government write the checks makes good sense (which is not to say that they should not be scrutinized and adjusted, to ensure that they are set on a sound actuarial footing).

But in the years since the New Deal, we have gone much further in introducing government funding and direction into social programs of all sorts, extending Rubinow's logic about the inadequacy of charity to all sorts of social services historically operated and supported philanthropically. We have, in the process, reduced the independence of philanthropy and the organizations that it supports and have set the stage for calls to limit that independence further.

The Great Society and the War on Poverty of the 1960s led not only to expanded social-insurance programs – notably, the Medicare health care program for the elderly – but also to a greatly expanded role for the federal government in subsidizing social-services programs of all kinds. The Urban Institute estimated in 2010 that "federal, state, and local government agencies have about 200,000 formal contracts and grant agreements with about 33,000 human-services groups that total $100 billion." What had been philanthropically-supported work, at the time that Warner wrote, was now deeply supported by the government, which decided what to fund and what the priorities should be.

Just as Rubinow had criticized what he saw as the limitations of private charity, this significantly different, new stage in the role of philanthropy – one in which it was becoming less independent and more a partner to government – had important intellectual champions, as well.

Most prominently, Johns Hopkins University political scientist Lester Salamon articulated the idea that without government funding to augment what private charity had traditionally done, programs to help those in

Although the government might assume that by directing funds to nonprofit institutions, it extends their reach without changing their character, that's likely not the case.

need would never have an adequate reach. Salamon coined such terms as *philanthropic insufficiency* and *philanthropic paternalism* – the view that those in need should not have to be or feel dependent on the wealthy because they "have a claim to assistance as a right." Salamon describes the shortcomings of philanthropy overall as "voluntary failure" – a term that, like the term "market failure," seems to indicate a need for government involvement, lest social services otherwise prove insufficiently funded and inadequate for their task.

It's a short step from such criticisms to the

view that private giving – whether via individual philanthropy or giving to foundations – should be a partner of government, to the point of funding the same organizations that the government does. Such a partnership, in which nonprofits that are partially supported by donations but also rely on government contracts, has been described as "third-party government," and it has, since the 1960s, reshaped the nonprofit and philanthropic landscape. As a result, government spending on such social services actually has come to surpass private giving – but goes often to the same agencies that private donors support. For instance, the Administration for Children and Families disburses some $50 billion annually for social-services providers; Giving USA reports that in 2011, private philanthropy in total directed $35 billion of private charitable contributions to human-services organizations, such as food pantries or homeless shelters.

It is, of course, entirely within the discretion of independent philanthropists whether to involve themselves in such arrangements.

But there is good reason to doubt whether this sort of government-led partnership often leads to good results. For instance, one of the most widespread of such public-private social-services programs, the preschool program for disadvantaged students known as Head Start, is provided, at a cost of $8 billion annually, in all 50 states by nonprofit groups, which can draw on both public and private sources of financial support. Yet a January 2010 report by the U.S. Department of Health and Human Services called "Head Start Impact Study," which compared Head Start participants with a control group, found that virtually all gains in vocabulary, math, and other skills realized by Head Start children had dissipated by the time the students had completed the first grade. A December 2012 follow-up report largely confirmed these results (though it found that some benefits lasted until the third grade).

To Isabel Sawhill of the Brookings Institution and Jon Baron of the Coalition for Evidence-Based Policy, the 2010 report demonstrated that the program "had almost no effect on children's cognitive, social-emotional, or health outcomes at the end of 1st grade." This may say as much about the unsolved challenge of how to use preschool education to help disadvantaged children as it does about public-private partnerships. But it's clearly the case that involving nonprofit groups did not really solve the problem of "voluntary failure." Nor were these disappointing results an isolated failure: Sawhill and Baron note that the Head Start study "is the 10th instance since 1990 in which an entire federal social program has been evaluated using the scientific 'gold standard' method of randomly assigning individuals to a program or control group. Nine of those evaluations found weak or no positive effects."

Such results should not be surprising. Although the government might assume that by directing funds to nonprofit institutions, it extends their reach without changing their character, that's likely not the case. As Steven Rathgeb Smith and Michael Lipsky observe in *Nonprofits for Hire*, the government "gradually influences the behavior of independent nonprofit contractors to accept its practices and preferred policies," and "[m]any volunteers, disillusioned with the changes in the organizations, simply leave." This is a recipe for what we so often see provided by government, as with Head Start: services that are extensive but mediocre. It is the sort of result that Amos Warner anticipated in the late 19th century, when he wrote, of the more limited public charities of his day, "In public charities, officialism is even more pronounced than under private management. The degradation of character of the man on a salary set to the work of relieving the poor is one of the most discouraging things in connection with relief-work, and it may be that public officials are especially liable to become hard and unsympathetic."

The argument can be made that there is inherent value in simply providing the services, regardless of the lack of any clear longer-term results. But surely, based on the disappointing results of the new era of government funding of previously independent nonprofits, one cannot conclude that such partnerships should be the *only* manner in which nonprofit "intermediary" organizations and their charitable partners work. Yet that is what another emerging school of thought – the latest to chip away at the idea of philanthropic independence that held sway in the era of Warner or de Tocqueville – seems to hold. This school of thought would have the purposes of government and philanthropy even more closely aligned – to the point that the income-tax code might be a vehicle with which to pick and choose the forms of philanthropy that should or should not be encouraged.

Indeed, serious calls have increased for the government to curtail the independence of philanthropy and charitable giving by playing an explicitly evaluative and directive role. Such thinking reflects suspicions that the federal tax code, through the charitable deduction, is effectively endorsing and advancing private purposes. Central to such criticism is the idea of the tax expenditure – first advanced in 1967 by Stanley S. Surrey, a former assistant secretary of the Treasury and Harvard Law School faculty member – which sees taxes reduced through legal deductions of any kind, whether the charitable tax deduction or the mortgage-interest deduction, as federal tax revenue forgone. Indeed, Surrey argued that the tax code had become a "vast subsidy apparatus to reward favored constituencies or subsidize narrow policy areas." His identification of the charitable tax deduction as one example of a tax expenditure has provided fuel for critics of private philanthropy.

The political scientist Rob Reich, director of Stanford University's Program in Ethics and Society (not to be confused with Robert Reich, a professor of public policy at the University of California, Berkeley), has, notably, argued that true philanthropy is, by definition, a force for reducing inequality. Reich, too, calls the charitable tax deduction a "subsidy," one that, moreover, may imply a role for government in directing private charitable giving. He offers a way to assess the value of that for which tax revenue is forgone: "Do public policies governing philanthropy contribute to activities in the form of direct assistance or structural reform that benefits the poor and disadvantaged? Do public policies direct or provide incentives for philanthropic dollars to flow in a redistributive direction, from rich to poor?" Reich concludes that the policy

---

Totalitarian societies do not encourage or even permit the independent institutions of civil society – whether churches, private schools, or even block associations.

---

that makes the charitable tax deduction available to donors providing support for any and all bona fide nonprofit groups is "remarkably indifferent to equality and redistributive outcomes." Nor does he spare religious giving –

which accounts for 32 percent of all U.S. charitable giving – from criticism: "Gifts to religious organizations can only be understood as predominantly for the operation and sustenance of the religious group and, in this sense, religious groups look more like mutual benefit societies than public charities. It appears very difficult, then, to construe giving to religion as redistributive." Religious institutions, thus, can be understood to have value for the society only to the extent that they operate soup kitchens, homeless shelters, and such. The community created by the institution itself is understood by Reich to be merely something that its financial supporters are enjoying for themselves.

The views of Reich and others have begun to take hold. The National Committee for Responsive Philanthropy, originally organized in 1976 to encourage foundations, in particular, to help "equalize the uneven playing field which decades of economic inequality and various forms of pervasive discrimination had created," has, through its executive director, Aaron

Dorfman, branded the charitable tax deduction as a "subsidy" for tax-exempt beneficiaries of privileged donors' choosing. Not surprisingly, Dorfman has also pushed for tax increases generally, partly to help support the sort of social programs toward which he thinks that charitable giving, as well, should be directed. His advocacy for "social-justice philanthropy," which is directly aimed at the needs of the poor, rather than, for instance, at museums and universities, has found resonance in Congress. There, Xavier Becerra (D-Calif.), a member of the House Ways and Means Committee (which is responsible for initiating changes to the tax code), has said of the charitable tax deduction, "Statistics I've seen suggest that only 1 in every 10 dollars are serving poor people or disadvantaged people. I have to wonder where the other 9 dollars are going."

It is accurate to say that wealthy taxpayers who itemize their tax deductions are those who disproportionately avail themselves of the charitable tax deduction. It is quite another to say that they "benefit" from giving their money away to charitable causes. It is but a short step from such views to the idea that there should be a limiting of the charitable tax deduction to select types of giving, judged – by legislation or IRS rule-making – to benefit, by some standard, those most in economic need.

The Obama White House has not gone that far to date. But it has moved consistently in a direction that would, almost without a doubt, reduce the extent of individual, independent philanthropy. Specifically, it has proposed, every year since 2009, that the value of the tax deduction for charitable giving be capped at 28 percent of the value of the gift, even for those taxpayers whose marginal tax bracket is at the highest rate of 39 percent. It's clear that the Obama administration sees such a limitation as a matter of fairness. Because the wealthy are the most likely to itemize their tax deductions and thus avail themselves of the charitable tax deduction, it is a matter of tax equity that their taxes not be reduced in ways the less affluent can't employ. The proposal ignores the fact, however, that if adopted, charitable giving will likely decline, according to Indiana University's Center on Philanthropy, by a billion dollars or more. The implicit White House assumption is this: that government can make better use of such funds.

Another Obama administration initiative embodies a related idea – that of government as the agenda-setter for private philanthropy. The Social Innovation Fund asks private donors to provide matching funds for federal grants to groups selected on the basis of priorities set by the federal Corporation for National and Community Service. The fund focuses on policy areas in the private social-services tradition: "economic opportunity, healthy futures, and youth development." Government grants come first; private philanthropy is asked to follow. Although advertised as a vehicle for identifying the most innovative and effective new social-service ideas – and using a combination of public and private funds to bring them "to scale"– in practice, the fund has worked with a handful of major foundations, which have provided matching funds and distributed small grants to hundreds of organizations, even including government agencies, in more than 30 states. It looks, in other words, to be an initiative that risks politicizing philanthropy. This theme – that government and philanthropic spending should be coordinated for maximum impact – could be heard in a February 2013 speech in Chicago, in which President Obama advanced the idea that to improve low-income neighborhoods, we should bring "all the resources to bear in a coordinated fashion so that we can get that tipping point where suddenly a community starts feeling like things are changing and we can come back."

In short, policy thinking has continued to move further and further away from support for independent philanthropy.

One does not have to believe that private giving can or should replace all government social programs to believe that it is, nonetheless, a vital force in American society, and thus one that should continue to have the unfettered discretion that it has historically enjoyed. A century of policy change has significantly narrowed the scope and range of independent philanthropy in America – and has seen a series of arguments arise against it. For reasons of principle and practicality, it deserves a defense.

IN DEFENSE OF INDEPENDENT PHILANTHROPY

A Beacon for Democracy

One must begin the defense of independent philanthropy with a defense of political pluralism – specifically, the opportunity for those whose view of the world is not that of the political majority to have a means for those views to have form. Such minority expression takes the form of donations of money or time in support of ideas and organizations embodying those values. James Madison, in defending his vision of a republic rather than a direct democracy, wrote (in "Federalist No. 10") of what might happen when "[a] common passion or interest will ... be felt by a majority of the whole ... and there is nothing to check the inducements to sacrifice the weaker party."

The organizations of civil society – supported by charity, not tax dollars – can be a safety valve for relieving tensions that can arise between majority and minority points of view. Madison clearly feared that in the absence of such safety valves, democracy might not long survive, lest those aggrieved by the direction set by the majority reject the legitimacy of the social order yet lack peaceable means of influencing its direction. Madison drew from a British tradition captured well by Lord William Beveridge, who wrote that through voluntary action, "human society may become a friendly society – an Affiliated Order of Branches, some large and many small, each with its own life in freedom."

Such organizations are a distinguishing feature of free societies – indeed, an aspect of liberty itself. Totalitarian societies do not encourage or even permit the independent institutions of civil society – whether churches, private schools, or even block associations. Nor do they recognize the property rights central to the disposition of assets via philanthropy. Put another way, independent philanthropy and the organizations that they support can be understood as forms of democratic speech, not just providers of services and assistance. And, of course, they are free to disagree with each other in pursuit of divergent goals.

In this context, the charitable tax deduction can also be understood in a different way. Rather than being seen as a subsidy, it can be viewed as a general expression of approval for civil society overall and for a free and decentralized approach to discussing and doing something about social problems – or simply supporting nongovernmental institutions. One cannot ignore the fact that, although the charitable tax deduction reduces a taxpayer's liability, it in no way enriches those who are donating – they, of course, receive no additional income. The tax code is sending a message that recognizes that not all that is good, effective, or even worth trying begins with government. In this context, the non-judgmental character of the charitable tax deduction is crucial to its combination of practical and symbolic importance. One could imagine a different perspective on this matter, were philanthropy consistently associated with a small set of ideas and approaches. But this is hardly the case. What Liza Hayes Percer has termed "ideational philanthropy" has provided support for both right-of-center (John M. Olin) and left-of-center (George Soros) institutions.

The charitable tax deduction can be viewed as a general expression of approval for civil society overall and for a free and decentralized approach to discussing and doing something about social problems.

Apart from the direct role that philanthropic and volunteer-supported organizations play, they strengthen democracy further by creating the "social capital" that arises, especially when volunteers come forward to found and support organizations. Because they are neither part of the government nor completely private, they are vehicles through which the capacity to help friends and neighbors – and enjoy their company – is forged. They are what Edmund Burke described as "little platoons" – associations that have since been found to protect against the anomie and alienation of modern society (although this was, to be sure, not Burke's focus). Such intermediary organizations provide the platform for more than 62 million Americans to volunteer their time each year in some way, many through nonprofits too small (under $25,000 in annual revenue) to be required to file with the Internal Revenue Service. There are well over a million such organizations. It's a phenomenon akin to voting – choosing from a wide range of candidates seeking support. As the political scientist Robert Putnam wrote in his famous monograph "Bowling Alone: America's Declining Social Capital," a deep civil society – characterized by many small community organizations – generates social capital, the groundwork of healthy societies, characterized by "social trust." "For a variety of reasons," he writes, "life is easier in a community blessed with a substantial stock of social capital."

Although Putnam's focus is on civil society's associations, not philanthropy, per se, it is clearly the case that the Tocquevillian associations that Putnam praises rely on decentralized dispersion of funds – in other words, private charity in the form of both money and time. Put another way, the benefits of the combination of mass philanthropy and mass volunteering weave a social fabric of trust and mutual aid that characterizes healthy societies. So it is shortsighted to understand philanthropy not directed at the immediate needs of the poor as necessarily serving the interests of the wealthy. But to understand fully why that is so, one must look as well at the character of giving and its effects.

Philanthropic Imagination and Effectiveness

Although Lord Beveridge defended philanthropically supported organizations as manifestations of freedom, he was, ironically, also the architect of the postwar British welfare state. Its proponents, like their counterparts in the United States, believed that government could be a larger version of the "friendly society" – one's neighbors, community, or coreligionists – but endowed with more assured resources and promising greater reliability. The British sociologist T. H. Marshall, for instance, wrote that publicly supported social services could be seen as "the entire citizen body organized in a great mutual aid society. All contribute and all are entitled to receive benefits. There is no longer any distinction between the privileged and the unprivileged." So it is that one sees the emergence of the idea that government and philanthropy can become one, in the service of creating a more perfect democracy, enabled by income redistribution.

Unfortunately, advocates of such a merger usually fail to distinguish between social-services programs – whether the tutoring of disadvantaged children or the provision of foster care for the abused – and programs that redistribute income. As suggested above, the government can do a reasonably effective job at the former but has shown great difficulty with the latter. The U.S. Department of Labor, for instance, administers some 47 job-training programs, at a cost of $18 billion annually. The largest of these, the Workforce Investment Act Adult Program, provided services to 7.2 million people in 2011, typically through private nonprofit contractors, but managed to place only slightly more than half (56 percent) in jobs – and almost 20 percent of those lost those positions within six months. It is worth comparing such results with those of a private, independent job-preparation program for people of low income, Cincinnati Works, which was founded and is still led by its two principals, retired accountant Dave Phillips and his wife, Liane, the author of a book-length exposition of an approach to helping the long-term unemployed *(Why Don't They Just Get a Job? One Couple's Mission to End Poverty in Their Community)*. The program eschews government funding. Its approach focuses on instilling habits and attitudes that lead to success in the workplace. The program reports that some 84 percent of those it has helped place in jobs from 2005 to 2012 continue to be employed, either in the job in which they were placed or in another.

The difference between Cincinnati Works and the world of government contractors is the difference between the individualized and the bureaucratic. The successful social-services group must specialize in personalized, "high touch" attention – the sort that successful businesses understand well in dealing with customers.

Amos Warner anticipated this specific

dynamic. Writing in 1894, he observed, "The State is not inventive, its agencies are not adaptable." Although, he wrote, "it is capable of doing a large, expensive work when the methods for doing it are sufficiently elaborated and standardized," he warned against the state's being involved in assistance that "cannot easily be reduced to a routine; [that] requires a degree of individualization of applicants rarely found in the conduct of public offices."

This leads logically to the conclusion that there are problems from which the government should steer clear, for which its greater reach will not lead to actual grasp. Such problems are better left to independent nonprofits that must compete for the support of private donors by running an honest and effective organization. Such groups can, moreover, replicate their successes through sister organizations in other locales. Indeed, Cincinnati Works is working with groups in 20 other cities to emulate its job-readiness program. In much the same way, the Boston-based group Village to Village Network is helping the elderly remain in their own homes in 93 additional locales, and St. Louis's The Mission Continues is helping veterans in 43 states adjust to civilian life. Although the federal government has supported church groups and others helping refugees find employment, a purely privately funded group, Upwardly Global, with offices in Chicago, Miami, New York, and San Francisco, decided to concentrate on refugees with professional skills and backgrounds who, it noticed, were not being well served by existing programs. Every year since 2001, the Manhattan Institute has identified non-governmental groups led by such "social entrepreneurs" overcoming difficult social problems and has given them cash awards for doing so. The spread of good ideas may not, in other words, require government partnership in order to bring them "to scale."

This case for the imagination and effectiveness of privately supported institutions in taking on the problems of the disadvantaged should not imply that other sorts of independent philanthropy are indulgences of the rich – self-interested investments, subsidized by taxpayers, and without benefits for the poor. A critic of private charity, Ken Stern, has argued along these lines in his 2013 book, *With Charity for All: Why Charities Are Failing and a Better Way to Give,* whichcriticizes gifts to elite universities and museums and "fashionable charities like the Central Park Conservancy."

The benefits of the combination of mass philanthropy and mass volunteering weave a social fabric of trust and mutual aid that characterizes healthy societies.

The assumption that only philanthropy that directly provides services to the poor is of benefit to them ignores a great deal. Do we think that medical research benefits only the rich? Do we think that universities that identify (and may reduce the tuition payments for) the most promising students from disadvantaged backgrounds serve only the affluent? Or that businesses established by their graduates and the products that they make are reserved for those of means? One must take a blinkered view of the effects of philanthropy to believe that its benefits are reserved for only a few. Spending on great educational institutions, libraries, and botanical gardens benefits everyone. A more humane, more thoughtful society is the result. Support for such institutions reflects the choices of elites, perhaps, but of elites who, in a democracy, feel compelled to take account of the common good. More broadly, here lies the essential flaw in the argument of Reich, Dorfman, Stern, and Becerra about philanthropy and the poor. Just as one can never tell which low-income student will be inspired by a visit to a museum, so is it impossible to know what the indirect benefits of philanthropic giving will be for society as a whole. During the depths of the

Depression, when my father visited Philadelphia's science museum, the Franklin Institute – originally the product of a philanthropic bequest from Benjamin Franklin – he was inspired to a life in science and engineering, a career that provided benefits to the broader society. Surely, the fact that the institute did not limit its programs to the disadvantaged or divert some portion of its resources to create a food pantry should not disqualify it from being viewed as an entity that offers potential benefits to the disadvantaged – who cannot afford private science tutors.

Changing Social Norms

All these groups propound more than just a method of service; they are associated with particular values. They are, it can be said, engaged not just in the delivery of services but in symbolic speech. They are sending a message about ways to live and ways to help others – and even why some others need help. Consider an organization that has become one of the most prominent nonprofits in the U.S. over the past 25 years. Teach for America (TFA), founded in 1990 by Wendy Kopp as an extension of an undergraduate project at Princeton, has recruited some 28,000 graduates of elite American colleges and universities to devote two years to teaching in public schools in low-income neighborhoods where students have done poorly.

TFA organizes recruitment and training assignments and has become a much sought-after position for new college graduates. The organization is doing more than recruiting top talent to help teach the disadvantaged – as important as that is. Rather, it's also speaking symbolically – in effect, saying that the existing system of teacher preparation through graduate schools of education is either ineffective or unnecessary and that public school systems are not, by themselves, up to the task of recruiting or retaining the teacher talent they need.

Kopp was motivated by her concern about a social problem – and a desire to make a statement, through her organization's activities, about an unconventional way to approach that problem. The character of her success is well captured by Smith and Lipsky, who write, "Nonprofit organizations represent different values from those held by government. They are free to take action without giving thought to the needs of the entire society or being under constraints of taxpayer preferences. They need not standardize their products. They can do things government cannot do." Private programs growing out of the values held by their inventors – and imbued with those values – can have an impact on society's norms more generally. In this sense, the good that private philanthropy does far transcends the good that it does for its immediate recipients.

There are ample examples of the influence of independent philanthropy and intermediary organizations on American norms. The early 20th century settlement-house movement, with independent outposts across the country, not only offered English classes for immigrants and fresh-air camps for their children but also promoted immigrant assimilation, or the Americanization of newcomers. The all-volunteer Alcoholics Anonymous, organized around locally directed chapters, not only helps individuals with drinking problems but successfully promotes the broad concept of self-help. Similarly, the early 1960s saw the growth and spread of preschools modeled on the methods of Italian educator Maria Montessori, from one to more than 3,000 locations, under the loose umbrella of the American Montessori Society, itself a nonprofit, which accredits Montessori teachers. It is not a stretch to say that their spread invigorated the general idea of serious early-childhood education. Indeed, as Amos Warner observed, "The best introduction a charity can have to the benevolent people of the community is the gradual diffusion from one intelligent person to another of the opinion that the charity is in fact doing something that is worthwhile."

A dramatic contemporary example is that of the philanthropy of Peter Thiel, the PayPal and Facebook billionaire, who announced in September 2010 that he would pay $100,000 each to a dozen young adults under the age of 20 to forgo college in favor of pursuing an original entrepreneurial venture. The public response was to see his contest as a broader criticism of higher education. In the years since Thiel's announcement, during which he appeared on 60 *Minutes* and became better known beyond business circles, a widespread rethinking of the value of a college education occurred, after decades in which its value – especially its economic value – was taken for granted. Since then, a new skepticism has emerged, dwelling on such problems as the burden of student-loan debt and the use of tuition to fund mushrooming layers of university administration at the expense of teaching and research. There can be little doubt that the private success and sometime celebrity of major philanthropists add to their impact. They can be seen, as Matthew Bishop and Michael Green have written in *Philanthrocapitalism: How Giving Can Save the World*, as "hyper-agents," freed from the constraints of convention by great wealth and imbued with influence by their established reputations.

Influencing cultural norms can have a greater impact on how we live than social-services programs of ever expanding reach. Indeed, if the parents of Head Start children should conclude, as a result of exposure to new ideas and alternatives, that their own efforts at home would have more lasting impact on their children's development, then new, less costly institutional arrangements might ensue. Just as law enforcement can succeed only in an environment in which most people obey

---

Spending on great educational institutions, libraries, and botanical gardens benefits everyone. A more humane, more thoughtful society is the result.

---

the law, and the tax system can function only because most Americans willingly pay what they owe, institutions and practices that promote certain norms of behavior and the values they rest on are ultimately more important than programs that seek to repair holes in the social fabric. Here lies the heart of the rejoinder to Lester Salamon's view that only a marriage between the voluntary sector and government can reach all those in need. Through its influence on the norms of behavior, organizations supported by a combination of independent philanthropy and volunteers can, in fact, "go to scale." We cannot note with any certainty how many young Americans who were not participants in Teach for America itself were nonetheless inspired to become teachers because of the prestige and importance that the organization attached to such a choice. But certainly there were many.

How far has the U.S. actually moved away from the tradition of independent philanthropy that this Broadside seeks to defend? Although government funding has held steady at about 8 percent of total nonprofit revenues, some portions of the nonprofit sector – social services for the poor, in particular, as noted – have come to be deeply entangled with government. The fact that thousands of small, often local organizations remain independent of government does not mean that philanthropy overall is not under fire, as critics seek to rein in the use of the tax exemption, limit it to approved uses, or broadly delegitimize it as an indulgence of the rich.

Independent philanthropy can be justified for the ways that it ameliorates concrete problems. But its defense must not be narrowly utilitarian. It is not a stretch to say that philanthropy safeguards freedom itself by fostering a profusion of views and perspectives and the organizations that emerge from and propagate those perspectives. The Nobel laureate Amartya Sen has argued, in reflecting on the character of a truly developed society, that the narrow measures of income and economic growth should not be the means by which to judge individual happiness and fulfillment. Rather, he contends, freedom should be understood as an end in itself, the oxygen that allows us to thrive and to enjoy our lives. "Most fundamentally," Sen writes, "political liberty and civil freedoms are directly important on their own and do not have to be justified indirectly in terms of their effect on the economy." This is the ultimate rejoinder to those who would assert that philanthropy must be judged in terms of its effects on select groups and causes. The liberty to give, unconstrained and uncoerced, is an expression of freedom itself – and should be encouraged in whatever form it takes.

Copyright © 2013 by Howard Husock

First American edition published in 2013 by Encounter Books,
an activity of Encounter for Culture and Education, Inc.,
a nonprofit, tax exempt corporation.
Encounter Books website address: www.encounterbooks.com

Manufactured in the United States and printed on
acid-free paper. The paper used in this publication meets
the minimum requirements of ANSI/NISO Z39.48–1992
(R 1997) (*Permanence of Paper*).

FIRST AMERICAN EDITION

LIBRARY OF CONGRESS CATALOGING-IN-PUBLICATION DATA

Husock, Howard.
Philanthropy under fire / Howard Husock.
pages cm. — (Encounter broadsides)
ISBN 978-1-59403-738-2 (pbk. : alk. paper) —
ISBN 978-1-59403-739-9 (ebook)
1. Charities—United States. 2. Endowments—United States.
3. Philanthropism—Political aspects. I. Title.
HV91.H82 2013
361.70973—dc23
2013020030
10 9 8 7 6 5 4 3 2 1

SERIES DESIGN BY CARL W. SCARBROUGH